HIGH WHITE MOON

POEMS FROM THREE ISLANDS:
GUEMES, FIDALGO AND HONSHU

THELMA J. PALMER

ISLAND PUBLISHERS
ANACORTES, WASHINGTON

High White Moon
Poems from Three Islands: Guemes, Fidalgo and Honshu

Copyright ©2001, Thelma Palmer
All rights reserved. No part of this book may be reproduced without permission from the publisher. Inquiries should be addressed to Island Publishers, 5869 Section Avenue, Anacortes WA 98221.

Printed in Canada.
First printing.

Cover illustration, *Owl and Moon*, by Philip McCracken, 1960.

Library of Congress Cataloging-In-Publication Data
Palmer, Thelma
   High White Moon : poems from three islands : Guemes, Fidalgo, and Honshu/Thelma Palmer.
ISBN 0-9615580-9-1
1. Guemes Island (Wash.)--Poetry. 2. Fidalgo Island (Wash.)--Poetry. 3. Honshu (Japan)--Poetry. I. Title

PS3566.A543 H54 2000
8.11'.54--dc21

00-037038

Dedication

This book is dedicated to Evan Palmer and Austin Palmer, my grandsons, in the hope it will help them understand who they are and where they came from. May they always traffic with angels and other potent spirits.

Acknowledgments

With thanks to Delphine Haley, my forever friend and business partner "whose wit is such harmonious madness;" to James Bertolino, poet and mentor, who can always be counted on—"as dependable as gravity;" and to Dixon Elder, comforter, who picks me up when I fall on my face "and never asks a crumb of me."

A special thanks to Philip McCracken for the cover, a linoleum block print from his early student days. It has an innocence and wonderment that makes me smile and say, "Ah, yes." Also, a special thanks to Anne McCracken who has always supported not only her husband's work but the arts in general—especially poetry.

Contents

Dedication 3
Acknowledgments 4

SECTION I: GUEMES ISLAND POEMS 9
High White Moon 10
And There Are Tremors In The Moon 11
Guemes Island Retirement Poem 12
A Synchronicity While Waiting For The Ferry 14
The Amazing Prince 16
Jonah's Near Death Experience 17
Looking Back 18
Bowing to God Light 19
Garden Credo 20
In A Field Of Daisies 21
Benediction 21
Summer Sting I 22
Summer Sting II 22
Queen Anne's Lace 23
Cormorant Crucifixes 24
Blue Heron On Fire 25
The Albino Bat 26
Cooper's Hawk 27
The Crossing-Over Place 28
Morning Gull 29
Hunger 30
Winter Gray With A Touch Of Red 31
Guemes Island Winter 32
Owl Call As Heard By The Scientist And The Mystic ... 33
Slow Horse Down The Road 34
A Bouquet Of Guemes Poets 35
A Ringing Of The Water Bell 36

SECTION II: FIDALGO ISLAND POEMS 37
The Tool Shed At Lake Campbell 38
The Whistle, The Barrow, The Magic 39
Father 40
Song For A Dead Child 41
Washing Machine At Lake Campbell 42
Photograph 43
Watering The Porch Boxes 44
Separating The Milk 45
Mother's Prescription For Grief Or Anger 46
Water, Milk And Paper Dolls 48
Note of Advice
   To The Good Nurse, Death 49
Going Home 50
If Only They Could Speak 51
My Mother's Hair 52
Generations 53
Walking The Sky Bridge 54
Mother Said Jesus Never Fails 55
Norwegian Watch Cap 56
Small Red-Eyed Bird 57
Spots 58
Wishes For A Grandson On His First Day Of School ... 59
Innocence And Oneness In Eden 60

SECTION III: DARRELL POEMS 61
Summer Song For A Sunburned Husband 62
For The Fisherman In This House Who Doesn't
   Care All That Much For Poetry Or Yoga 63
Hindsight 64
The Male Ego 64
A Rat Tale 65
Distance: Three Views 66
Rite Of Purification 67
Jack Island, December 68

The Rose 69
It's All In Knowing Where To Look Before Death ... 70
Long Before Dawn 71
Some Rites And A Sacrament For Darrell 72
Points Of View 74
Loneliness 75
Kettle Burn 76
Who Are You Tells Me This Dream 77
For The Sake Of Grace 78
Wounding 78
Transformation 79
Letting Go 80
Rose Metaphor 81
For Darrell Who Trafficked With Angels 82

SECTION IV: HONSHU ISLAND POEMS 83
The Rabbit In The Moon 84
Izumi 85
Izumi Tells Masaaki About American Parents ....
    Catching Guemes Ferry 86
On Entering the Kingdom of Heaven 87
On Becoming An Empress 88
On Visiting Peony Priest a Second Time 89
Speaking Zen On Reflection 90
Watching Otoasan Tend Bonsai 91
Japanese Women And Their Sons 92
Woman As Hare 93
Learning About Heaven 94
Two Women Under Cherry Blossoms 95
Biography 96

HIGH WHITE
MOON

Section I

Guemes Island Poems

In 1980 Darrell and I moved to Guemes Island for what we expected would be one year. For a time I would have the isolation and quiet to write, and then we would return to Fidalgo Island. That single year has stretched into twenty.

We fell in love with this place. With the quiet people who live back in the woods and pay attention to the seasons and phases of the moon. With the folks who live along the road and wave when you pass. With the painters, sculptors, musicians and writers who find the laid-back lifestyle conducive to their art. With the dogs that sleep in the middle of the road. With Guemes road etiquette which never allows one car to overtake another on the way to the ferry.

No matter that trees regularly fall across wires and leave us without electricity. Candles and firelight are soothing and easier on the eyes anyway. And if no one comes from the mainland by six o'clock in the evening, we are home free because the last ferry has come and gone for the day.

There's a community hall, church, library, playground, firehall and cemetery—but no jail. More recently a single store that sells feed for our chickens in addition to groceries and gas.

God bless Guemes and the Wood Choppers Ball.

High White Moon

Tonight the moon is a ghost
the size of my thumb.

Thin as a transparent wafer,
it would melt on my tongue
like Eucharist.
Holy. Holy.

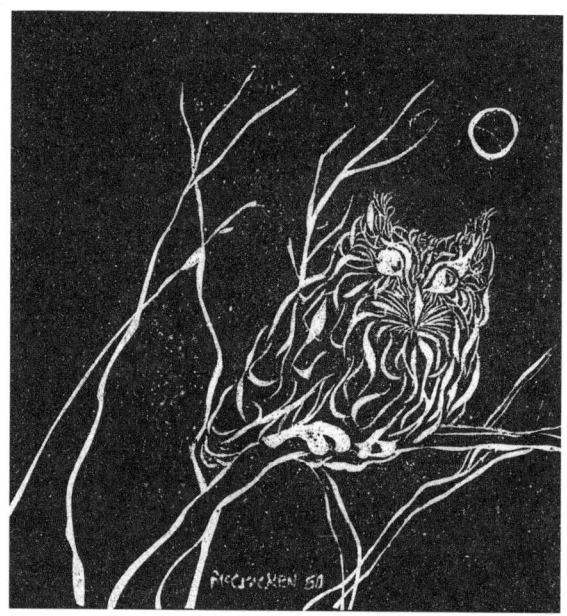

Owl and Moon
—Print by Philip McCracken

And There Are Tremors In The Moon

When so much as one dry leaf
drops from the high branch
and slips softly downward
on napping autumn air,
the whole earth sighs and susurrates,
and suns in distant galaxies
adjust their flare.

When one small rabbit dies
to the tearing claws and beak
of some hungry hawk at noon,
the whole universe recalculates
and there are tremors in the moon.

Guemes Island Retirement Poem

I
Dusted the chickens for mites and lice,
dipped their legs in crankcase oil
and painted the roosts with disinfectant.

Helped Darrell dig up
the plugged and broken septic line
between the grease trap and drain field.

Shelled peas
under the pie-cherry tree
scaring off would-be robin robbers,
picked cherries and raspberries,
then froze and pied.

Gathered seaweed
and strung it out on logs to dry
for winter garden.

Prayed to Gaia
before Darrell cut down the young fir.
New space opens to blue spruce not seen before
and new water perspectives.

Trimmed the roses, tied the phlox,
cut the grass, trimmed the roses,
hoed the garden, checked the pool,
cut the grass, pulled the weeds,
thinned the beets
 and

HIGH WHITE MOON

II
oh
heard the birds
and the soft whispering
of growing things
and
floated gently as a lily
on baptismal water
purified
and
smelled the pungent woods
newly ferned and nettled
four dogs following to the mailbox

III
The sun rises,
the sun sets,
the moon and stars.
What was that thing called "clock?"

Rain
the ticking of the aspen leaves.

I hear there is a ferry
from this island to another place.

I don't believe it.

A Synchronicity While Waiting For The Ferry

(When a physicist is needed, a physicist appears.)

Reading *Chaos: Making A New Science*,
wishing I could talk to a physicist about "turbulence"
and "strange attractors,"
I get out and stroll downhill
past waiting cars toward the beach.

It is September, Indian summer,
eerily still and warm. No breath of air,
just sun bathing the island with golden light,
and one last butterfly floating above
the roadside asters.

"Great weather," I say in passing
the open windows of neighbors who lean out
and call after me, "Yes, but my garden could use rain."
Or, "I hope it lasts all month."

I do not know the gray-haired man
in the California van, but I speak anyway.
"Isn't this weather great!"
"I just finished it," he calls out as I go by.
"What?" I think, then stop as though—
and turning back in astonishment inquire,
"You just finished it?"
"And it wasn't all that good," he replies, indicating
a book about radio disturbance on his dash.
"I write about disturbance myself," he continues.
"Is that like turbulence?" I wonder out loud.
And then we have this amazing conversation
about ships during World War II and Murmansk,

HIGH WHITE
MOON

and the Aleutian Islands, and the "Butterfly Effect,"
and "strange attractors,"
and disturbance which is like turbulence
which is like randomness which is like chaos.
And he turns out to be a physicist
retired from UC Berkeley, and then the ferry has come,
and I whack my palm against my forehead and
exclaim,
"All this because I said, 'Isn't this weather great'!"
"Oh, I thought you asked 'Why aren't you reading a
book?' "
Confused, our eyes meet as if for the first time,
and, falling into chaos,
we can do nothing but repeat ourselves.

"Isn't this weather great?"

"I just finished it."

Crossing the channel I ride outside on the bow
gazing into green autumn water
flinked with butterflies of sunlight.
Somewhere behind me that guy,
that "strange attractor,"
is sitting alone in his van,
and I am careful not to look back.

—For Bob Brown

HIGH WHITE
MOON

THE AMAZING PRINCE

Prince, his wife dead, sons raised,
is retired from the mill,
and grows an outrageous garden.
Sells the best firewood the cheapest,
shaves once a week,
and has no front teeth.

Dickering with him, one day, for cedar posts,
he told me he'd used the same bean poles
for forty years.
 I was circling slowly in the mystery of him
glimpsing dark pockets of glitter,
when a weedy young woman
in a green print dress
crossed the road toward us.
She walked straight up to Prince,
looked him hard in the eye,
flicked the brim of his dirty red hat,
and kissed him on the lips.

Prince said something I couldn't hear,
she smiled
and slipped past us into the orchard.

Crossing the Strait today,
I saw Prince
fishing in his aluminum boat
so narrow an orca would swamp him
with a good tail smack.
Prince, in his old red hat,
gets more halibut than most,
and I imagined
a white-winged fish of the migrating eye

circling his lure,
its sideways mouth
pumping water like salty kisses.

Jonah's Near Death Experience

His boat smashed in the storm,
Jonah managed alone till dark
in the raging sea.
Sputtered and flailed,
called God,
cursed God,
wanted to give up but could not.

When the whale came at last
and opened his monstrous maw,
Jonah swam in willingly,
latched onto an ivory tooth
and spent the night curled
on the soft pink tongue
in the blow and draw of stinking air.

Next morning, the mammoth
spat him onto the beach,
and Jonah, hugging himself,
rolled in the sand
and laughed and laughed.
Who could have guessed
God was a whale with bad breath.

Looking Back

We have been friends for thirty years,
through happiness and sadness over husbands,
mothers, children, students;
through grief at sickness and at death;
through joy in books and gardens;
driving small cars toward
some distant impossible perfection
that kept receding into *next* spring,
next fall, *next* Christmas.
Perhaps we can say, truly,
that the journey was more important
than the *never* getting there.

Perhaps we can say just as truly
that we have not journeyed at all,
but have always been rooted, here,
in the heart of that for which we searched.

—For Anne McCracken

Bowing to God Light

The sun is at my back,
the clearing just ahead through woods,
when suddenly upon the path appears
an oval patch of sunlight like a mirror
where my shadow falls.
 A voice beyond
some far horizon calls,
"*You* belong in sunlight, not your shadow."
And so I step into my darkest self,
embrace her as my own
and slowly turn to face the sun
which streams a blessing down.

The soft wet voices of cathedral trees
chant praise, their branches
reach out brushing me to bliss,
a bird bursts like a bell within my heart,
and I know beyond all words
the majesty enfolding me.

Then the way the water in the earth
draws down the willow in a witcher's hand,
a singing in the earth
bows down my head before the light.

Garden Credo

I believe in Gaia the Mother All-tender,
Earth Spirit, maker of gardens,
and in her sons and daughters,
the trees and plants of four seasons.
I believe in the white lilies
and red ranunculus of summer,
and in their seeds.
I believe in the pears and apples of autumn,
the pumpkins, the blue-gray squashes
that nourish our bodies with their meat,
our spirits with their beauty.
I believe in the holly of winter
whose needling leaves and red berries
unite the green of Gaia to the blood of Christ.
I believe in the crocus and tulips of spring
whose petals open like sacred chalices
 from which all may drink the joy of the garden.

In A Field Of Daisies

White daisies
float on slender stems
above the golden grass,
star the summer field
with dazzling little poems
from the universe
that will not let me pass.

Benediction

Bronze Buddha from Burma
sits lotused in my Northwest garden
above the pond,
beside the rhododendron bush.

Life-sized, patina-green and patient,
he meditates by sun and moon and stars,
through all the seasons of the year.

Today, a plump, red-legged frog
with bulging golden eyes
squats low and still
within the Buddha's upturned palms
receiving benediction.

Summer Sting I

Water,
waiting still and dark
in the deep well,
rises noiselessly
through secret pipes
to the bird bath
where it fountains crystal clear,
shimmers in early sun,
summons finches and siskins
to their morning splash
and the cat.

Summer Sting II

The tumbler pigeons,
white air-angels,
flop,
somersault,
fall earthward,
pretend to be shot,
so the hunter will stop firing.

Below,
waiting
at the entrance to the cote,
idly pecking spilled peas,
a Goshawk.

QUEEN ANNE'S LACE

Small white pillow face
tatted by summer's genius,
your intricate lace
is centered
with a single purple eye
that astonishes.

You are for singing
in the fragrant valley
of a woman's breasts.
For riding the cold mountains
of a dead Queen's eyes.

Cormorant Crucifixes

Cormorants float on logs,
hold wings wide to dry
in winter sun.

These black Christs
nailed to their own arms.

Blue Heron On Fire

Tall bird
at water's edge
hesitates to fly.

Waits
motionless
as though afraid.

Stands still
and waits
and waits
and waits

until
until
the Merciful of frightened birds
strikes courage
to her feathered heart.

Then
leaning
forward
slowly
onto silver air,
she glides across the bay,

rides the pure invisible
to Iona,
catching fire
along the way.

–for Delphine Haley

The Albino Bat

Just at dark, the albino bat
flattens herself,
squeezes thin as a leaf
from beneath cedar shakes,
opens like a cup-sized umbrella
and flies.

Darts past our windows—
an astonishment—
scooping bugs
in pale suede wings.

Watching and wondering, we exclaim,

"There she is! There she is!
See I told you. A white bat."

Maneuvering erratically,
veering and falling,
this creature of the night
outwits mosquitoes and small moths,
outwits our common sense
and speaks to something darker
in our hearts.

Back and forth she flies
until we sleep only to find
enigma has entered our dreams
upside down
peering at us with pink eyes—
blind.

Cooper's Hawk

Cooper's hawk arrows houseward
for a sparrow at the feeder.
Hunger rockets her at death-defying speed
through leafless winter tree,
and in an instant of miscalculation
as victim veers,
she crashes head-first into glass.

The dogs arrive before I do,
inquire tenderly with gentle noses
why this flying creature
lies so still upon the walk.
I, too, am filled with wonder,
as I hold the yet-warm supple hawk,
admiring the speckled feathering,
the long and broad-striped tail
that steered her to sure death.

And then in final bird goodbye,
a white transparent eyelid
closes slowly from the bottom up
across each shining eye.

THE CROSSING-OVER PLACE

Napping in the window seat,
I dream and soar—
a woman-hawk on icy air.

My blouse sleeves bubble, ruffle
in the winter wind; my hair sweeps back;
I rise and fall or drift away at will.

Called back into my body
by distant barking dogs,
I swoop across an arc of silver light

but pause beyond the glass,
not ready yet to enter self entirely.
Here within this crossing-over place

where I neither sleep nor wake,
I understand the cross of Banbury,
the cross of hot buns,

the "x" of the kiss,
and the cross of Christ.
Here where

Heloise and Abelard are at peace,
Sisyphus has his rock up the hill,
Prometheus is living fire,

here, Christ laughs
like a lotused Buddha,
and I almost get the joke.

Morning Gull

Morning, that great white gull,
swoops in through my window
on full-sail wings,
hovers overhead
between sleeping and waking,
mewing, "It's time! It's time!"

I am hesitant to choose morning
over the night palaces.
Over the rooms of my secret self
where pain is a silver blade
drawn through a heart
not quite my own,
where joy rings me like a bell
but through a silk curtain.

When gull shatters to glittering shards,
I choose this day,
or it chooses me.
No way to be certain.

Hunger

The great owl
unfolded
from her winter tree
and sailed
silently
to clearing's edge.

Hunger,
bone-white
and bright as a burning star,
moved her to risk
full daylight
for a mouse.

Winter Gray With A Touch Of Red

All the grays
of a Northwest winter.
The tin-foil gray
of bay water
beneath blue-gray clouds
that open and close
to a dove-gray sky.
The charcoal gray
of alder skeletons
along the lane
where we walked,
your gray glove nesting
my red.

Guemes Island Winter

For days,
it snowed and snowed,
large lacy flakes
lazing quiet down the sky,
small silver ices
stinging and incessant.

"Surely, tomorrow it will stop,"
we said.
But, no!
Something in the universe
was hell-bent for snow.

The garden Buddha grew
a fez,
 a scarf,
 a lap robe,
and the shrubbery disappeared
in icy igloo rounds.

And, still, it snowed and snowed
until we, too, were covered
past our lips,
our eyes,
our crowns:
two white mounds that leaned together
mummied in the snow.

—For William Fast

HIGH WHITE
MOON

OWL CALL
AS HEARD BY THE SCIENTIST
AND THE MYSTIC

Tonight on our walk,
you heard the great horned owl
call two times from the woods
and wished
you could count the vibrations,
measure the sound waves,
examine its pellets
for mice bones.

I heard that same owl
flute its mellow instrument
just once.
The second call was an answer
from a temple of trees
across the valley.

–For Dixon Elder

Slow Horse Down The Road

Why ride a horse at all
if you can't gallop

callop callop callop

hair flying
body leaning forward

callop callop callop

racing across fields
jumping ditches
careening corners
cold air biting your
laughing teeth

callop callop callop

crashing
breaking your leg
horse ok
riding on

callop callop callop

A Bouquet Of Guemes Poets

There are pods of whales
and gaggles of geese.
There are prides of lions
and moons made of cheese.

There are nides of pheasants
and flocks of goats,
but we are a bouquet,
a bouquet of poats.

We are catnip and fleabane,
pink pigsqueak and nettle.
We are sneezewort and goat's beard
where aphids won't settle.

We are bleeding hearts,
lambs ears and naked day lilies.
We are monks hood and prayer plants
and, sometimes, plain sillies.

We are heartsease and heal all
and heavenly roses,
eight bushes afire
burning brighter than Moses'.

—For James Bertolino, Dixon Elder, George Geanuleas,
David Gladish, Barbara Groves, Jackie Hartwich,
and Helen Trefethen

HIGH WHITE
MOON

A RINGING OF THE WATER BELL

Full-moon woman,
round sky clapper,
fell into the sea tonight
and somersaulting
in the silver wake
behind your small departing boat,
she rang the water bell.

SECTION II

FIDALGO ISLAND POEMS

Born at Lake Campbell on Fidalgo Island, I have always lived on islands. They are special places, isolated in a way, but surrounded by water that ultimately connects those who live on them to every other island, continent and ocean on earth.

I think of Fidalgo Island as a mandala whose center is Mount Erie—that great stone heart rising one thousand feet into the air and surrounded by seven lakes. Little Cranberry, Heart Lake, Lake Erie, Lake Campbell, Best Lake, Whistle Lake and Pass Lake.

My lake, Campbell, is a miniature mandala in itself because it circles the small island in its center known as Goat Island.

These poems are from a time of family and memory that remain in the heart.

My father, a hard working fisherman, who adored his children and grandchildren. My mother, a creative woman who dreamed a career of music that never could be.

At the end of this section are poems of children and grandchildren who, like islands themselves, are separate but connected.

The Tool Shed At Lake Campbell

Father and I work alone
in this universe of nails,
nickel-plated, rusted, bent;
in this place of screws and bolts,
of leather thongs.

Is the lake frozen?
Here there are clamp-on skates,
a dozen or more,
little ones and big ones.
We sharpen them,
oil away the rust, polish them,
leave them outside the door
for cousins.

Is there a hole in your shoe?
We will re-sole it
or put on a new heel.
We can punch holes in leather.

Hammers, saws,
a hatchet so dull
a little girl is allowed
to split kindling.
This room is a jumble of doing.
Father built caskets here,
makes porch boxes.

What we learn in this tool shed
is unsayable.
Drowning into rusty whirlpools of self,
we call out, "Love me, for God's sake.
Love me."

The Whistle, The Barrow, The Magic

Father cut me a whistle
from an alder sapling
and gave it to me saying,
"This is for whistling back birds
and other lost things."

Father built me a wheelbarrow,
painted it blue
and gave it to me saying,
"When whistling won't work,
cart with your barrow."

Father showed me magic
with three hats and four paper balls
and taught it to me saying,
"If whistling or carting won't do,
you may need to amaze."

Father gave me Mother's gold ring,
her lavaliere of smoke agate
and kissed me goodbye saying,
"Don't forget to be a woman."

Father

Father died slowly.
For seven days in January he lay
like Dylan's robin in the snow,
all but one of his fires out.
I nursed him
and let them fuel his one last fire
through tubes until so much of him
was flown away, my heart closed
down, and iron doors inside of me
cranked shut.

And I—that daughter
for whom he tapped sweet alder whistles,
charmed four paper balls beneath three hats—
that daughter,
went before the doctor-god and ordered,
"No more fuel. Take the needles out."

"Shall we wait until your brother comes?"

"No. Now. Take the needles out."

I sat beside his bed and held his hand
until his purl came slight as feather breath
and was no more.

Song For A Dead Child

My father comes to me in a dream,
rises up to the top as sweetly as cream,
lifts purely like moon singing out of the sea,
and he carries a dead child who looks just like me.
The small girl is wearing a comical dress
made of funnies and jokes and pleats without press,
and she's gone all stiff and feels quite cold
as he hands her to me to rock and to hold.

Then Father starts singing of wind in the trees,
of nissen and trolls, of mice made of cheese,
of dried purple violets kept in a jar,
of curved boats like new-moons that sail to a star.
He sings, now, of king apples, juicy and red,
of a child who sleeps in an apple-green bed,
of small silver bangles and pictures in lockets,
of candy surprises and agates in pockets.
He takes out his mouth harp; he whistles and flutes
the praises of willows, their leaves and their roots.
He tootles the tune of a sorrow upstairs
where a little girl cries and will not say her prayers.

And the dead child he brought me begins, now, to wake
in my arms, to stretch and to make
stirring sounds like an innocent creature just coming alive,
cooing sounds like a dove in the morning at quarter-of-five.

Then Father is gone, and I'm left with this child,
who's naughty and playful and more than a little bit wild.

Washing Machine At Lake Campbell

First Maytag at the lake!
Great excitement as we pull
the crate apart
and there she stands:
green short-skirted girl
with four skinny legs
and an electric wringer.

How dangerous!
Mother's long hair could be caught
between the rubber rollers,
her hands crushed,
and what of her breasts that swing
like bells?

We carry bucketsful of hot water
from the boiler in the kitchen,
add chips of homemade soap,
plug in the cord,
and stand back as this miracle
of rural electrification
tumbles water to suds.

Sheets, pillowcases, slips,
embroidered tea towels,
nightgowns, underwear,
and Father's work pants,
dip and dive effortlessly
in the enameled belly,
slip easily into tight wringer lips
that cascade small waterfalls
back into the machine.

Clean clothes blow on our line long before
any neighbor has hung out her wash.

And Mother is just fine.

Photograph

There is a photograph of my mother at eighteen
wearing a white tucked blouse
and a long black skirt.
She stands in the garden
holding an armload of lilies,
the way a pianist might hold
a gift of flowers at the end of a concert.
Unsmiling, she seems to be listening
to sad music that no one else hears.

Watering The Porch Boxes

My mother tended the porch boxes at night
after the garden and barn and kitchen work was done
and twilight had settled over our lake world.
I would stand beside her, unspeaking,
a young girl learning sadness
in the small clouds of fragrance
that rose from touched leaves and blossoms.
The pansies were velvet faces
with large and startled eyes close to weeping,
the petunias, soft mouths that licked our fingers
and breathed mauve songs into the evening.
Sometimes strange and exotic night creatures
came to us out of darkness,
great flying beetles, burgundy by moonlight,
and gentle scalloped moths
that wore blind eyes upon their wings.
My mother watched those skimming fliers as they floated
where they would beneath the stars, while
I listened to the nighthawks falling down the sky
and to her silence born of some ancient sorrow
that she could almost drown at close of day
in nighttides and in flowers.

Separating The Milk

Mother turns the handle
of the blue and silver machine
whirring a fine-meshed tune
as sweet milk in the high bowl
spins, whirls, concaves,
and thick cream streams
from the shiny spout.

Her straw hat
caught by a ribbon across her throat,
hangs down her back as she cranks
thoughtfully in blue smock
with rolled-up sleeves,
and I spin in the dark smells
of her hands that have
patted the cow's flank
and were wetted with milk
for the easier pulling of teats.

I am newly thirteen
and wait beside her with my
bowl of blackberries,
but she is scarcely aware of me.
She is here in this room,
separating milk from cream,
but she is also out there
in last light of evening
separating sorrow from dream.

Mother's Prescription For Grief Or Anger

Before breakfast:
fill the wood box,
(big chunks and bark to hold the fire),
hoe the beans and feed the chickens.

After breakfast:
invite six people to dinner
and trim the fir that reaches too far
into the field.
Clean the chicken pen,
spread manured straw around the cucumbers,
shove the boat down to the water
and row out to pull the crab trap.
Butcher seven crab, clean and carry them
back up the hill
along with a sackfull of seaweed for mulch.
Cook the crab and crack them.
It's time for lunch.

Spade hard in the afternoon—anywhere.
Stab the shovel into the earth
and shove like you are digging to Tibet.
Pick peas and dig potatoes for supper,
a few zucchini, raspberries, and the windfall summer apples.
Gather roses for the dinner table
and pull a few weeds while you are at it.
Feed the dogs and cat
and water the petunias before going in.

HIGH WHITE
MOON

Don't sit down during dinner.
Tell your guests you will sit down in a moment.
Say you have one more thing to do,
say you are not hungry,
say anything but keep moving
between the kitchen and the table.
Join them for coffee.
Laugh a lot and they won't know
that you really are not there,
but off remembering—floating somewhere
between heaven and earth—apple skins
stuck between your teeth
and something dead in your arms.

After dinner:
refuse help with the dishes.
Sweep the floor when they are gone,
wash clothes and put things away.
Tell any man who asks that you are not tired.
Keep moving; work past tired, and anger, and grief.
Before bed sit down with the cat
and stroke until she purrs.

If you have cared for everything
before yourself,
you *have* cared for yourself,
and you will be swept into minor-chord sleep
on that great subterranean river.

Water, Milk And Paper Dolls

Mother fell
and struck her head,
lay for fifteen hours in the tub
before we found her.
All speech gone,
she could only write notes
or wave from the hospital bed.

That night I dreamed a deep well
with just a little water in it,
and a milkweed hanging by one root
halfway down the side.

I dreamed that she and I
were paper dolls in flaring skirts,
ring-a-rosing near the edge.

Note of Advice
To The Good Nurse, Death

My mother will never die in the fall
because king apples need polishing then,
need peeling round and round
in one continuous skin for eating by the fire.

She would refuse to die in winter
because pussy willows bud in December,
and purple violets make promises
beneath brown leaves.

Nor would Mother let go of this earth
in spring when tulips and daffodils,
first swallows and asparagus
come to her garden.

Your only chance, Good Nurse, will be
to come for Mother in summer,
a cool drink in your hand,
a soothing salve in your apron pocket.

I've seen her fan herself
with her straw hat in August
beside the well when the water is low
and the deer flies are biting.

Going Home

When my mother got sick,
we moved her to town,
and now I take her for rides twice a week
out Mountain Road and past
the homes at Lake Campbell—
where our family has lived for a hundred years.
And though her speech is gone,
I know she loves the drive because
she nods and claps
as we creep around Heart Lake
and through the woods in her fifty-one Chevy.

So much of her spirit has left her body
that I can't be certain if she truly knows
the old places anymore:
the side road she walked to Anacortes
for piano lessons when she was twelve,
the house where I was born,
her parents' place, the crooked maple,
the island in the middle of the lake.
Sometimes I fantasize she will die
in the old car as we drive along.

Some days, I hope she will die
just as we crest the hill
going down to Uncle Emil's,
and then, she and I,
just the two of us, rolling along
sun-mottled under the maples,
can coast together
one last time toward home.

If Only They Could Speak

All speech gone,
Mother wrote notes that I still find
three years after her death.
A scrap of paper fallen behind a drawer
says: "These are my grandchildren."

Scrawled on an envelope
folded in her coat pocket:
"Spring is just around the corner."

Her last poem written on a recipe card
and found in the glove compartment
of her old Chevrolet:
"Roses in December
They try so hard to please.
There's so much that they remember
If only they could speak."

My Mother's Hair

By dream at night
I want to comb
my mother's hair.
She is alive and young again
like her picture at eighteen.
Her hair is fashioned high
on her head. Slowly,
I remove the tortoise-shell combs
and the crimped pins.

Long brown hair
cascades down her back
in a waterfall of light.

Generations

Speeding downhill
on a sled in snow,
the fence-posts blur
to paper dolls,
white-hatted,
holding barbed wire hands.

Mothers and their daughters
moving one into and through
the other,
kissing as they go.

Walking The Sky Bridge

Last night I met my mother walking a sky-bridge
that arched high above the world.
She was young and beautiful beyond words,
her head high, her back straight, her face calm
with a knowing born of suffering.
Her mouth knew the words,
but she did not speak to me.
Her eyes could see,
but she did not look at me because
she was in some resonant space
where there is no pain,
and we could not cross over to one another.

All I could do was call out three times in passing:
"She is my mother, and she is so beautiful!
Oh, my God! She is so beautiful.
She is my mother, and she is so beautiful."

Mother Said Jesus Never Fails

Stuck in the desert
I was dying until
I remembered mother said

call Jesus

Jesus

I cried

Jesus

And off in the distance
 a dust rose
and there He came
by bicycle
hair flying
robes flapping

Stopped so fast
in front of me
His back tire slid sideways
in sand

Climb on
He said
tapping the handlebars

Mother never said
I'd be in for the ride of my life.

Norwegian Watch Cap

This cap that I knitted for you
of thick wool
in love and daimon haste

is no ordinary hat. In one night
it grew in my hands like a mushroom.
It is a lyric poem for your head;

a proud blue topknot
cleverly tangled by Clotho;
a protective Viking helmet

that your grandfather sang
to my needles.
It is a bird with wings folded in yarn.

If you ever lose it, set out a live trap
with a gray mouse for bait,
and this cap will come flying.

—For Dennis Palmer

Small Red-Eyed Bird

At Christmas Island
a small red-eyed bird
attached to you aboard ship:
perched on the rim of your
morning coffee mug;
lit on the arm of your chair;
shared your melon at lunch;
even followed you ashore
to count coconut crabs.

That afternoon it settled
on your open map and shit
on the South Pacific.
You rolled your eyes
remembering the red-eyed towhee
your father was watching
the day he advised you
not to spend too much time
away from this valley
where your family has lived
for five generations.

—For Bradley Palmer

HIGH WHITE
MOON

Spots

When star-gazing lilies
start to open their buds,
you dream freckles and mottles,
skies speckled with birds.

Your nights are all peppered
with stipples and dots,
as you wait lily faces
to show you their spots.

—For Jan Hunt-Palmer who raises lilies.

Wishes For A Grandson
On His First Day Of School

May your feet leap and run
with the swiftness of Deer
and find their way through rocky places
with the surefootedness of Goat.

May you be wary as Mountain Lion,
trusting as Lamb
and may the eyes of Cat
guide you through dark nights.

May the wisdom of Owl
fill your heart
and the memory of Elephant
compute your arithmetic.

And like Coyote, who never
contemplates the shit on his tail,
may you show us the pads of your paws
as you race headlong
into mystery.

—*For Evan Palmer who said, "Grandma, I'm scared."**

---

* *Two days after the start of school, Evan and his mother happened to drive by LaConner Elementary. He sighed and said wistfully, "I wish I could live there."*

Innocence And Oneness In Eden

Grandson
airing in buggy
under November sun,
hears ravens quork,
sees robins
eat holly berries.

Unable to separate birds
from self,
he laughs out loud
and chortles,
overjoyed,
to be making
such hollow and outrageous noises,
to be gobbling red fruit
in green thorn.

—For Austin Palmer

Section III

Darrell Poems

Darrell fell in love with Guemes Island as much as I, and we were happy here for fourteen years when he was diagnosed with cancer. The following poems helped me siphon off the grief of his going and helped me heal.

During WWII his plane was going down in the Pacific Ocean, and in the ensuing chaos he glanced out the window and to his stunned amazement saw an angel riding on his wing. She was very puzzling to him because he was not a formally religious man. He wondered whether she had come to take him to heaven or to save him for earth. Rescued after floating around on a raft for 4 days, he never forgot that image though over the years he only spoke of it to closest family and friends.

His last days were spent here on Guemes looking across the water and watching the birds. Three days before dying he said, "My angel comes every morning now. Today she said, 'Now it's your turn.'"

A few days after his death, a dove, hawk-driven, smashed into the window where he had lain watching birds. The astonishing white print that appeared on the glass resembled a white angel with wings raised gracefully pointing out heaven.

Summer Song
For A Sunburned Husband

You laughed
saying your totem was an otter.
"Be serious," I said.
"Totems are important."

Besides, who could think
of a six-foot otter, pink,
floating face-up in the water
with a rock on his chest
for smashing clams?

But, when I lay my head
like a stone on your breast
trying to imagine the scene,
we floated off down-sea
smooth as two furred creatures
in a rolling ground swell.

For The Fisherman In This House Who Doesn't Care All That Much For Poetry Or Yoga

See how I struggle with words
positioning "North" around the page,
rhyming and scheming.
How I wait, lotused, breathing Prana,
hoping for showers of golden rain
to ecstaticize me like Theresa's arrows.

How wise you are; how good
at ritual and myth
and do not even know.

You lower your invisible line
into Black Rock's inverted atmosphere
where the halibut,
like white-winged water-birds,
maintain within wet air.
And there, some sea-girl with migrating eye
and a mouth that opens vertically like a vulva
snaps your bait.
And you reel her in,
or do you reel yourself into your own mythology?
You do not anguish for words,
but caress her with your knife,
your breath rising and falling.

Hindsight

Eve's only sin
was in not making applesauce,
smearing it all over Adam
and leaving him in the sun
to dry like fruit leather.

The Male Ego

When Jack Horner got cornered,
he investigated the plum
obliquely
under crust.

Sticking in his thumb
and pulling out a cooked fruit,
the little bastard
immediately assumed
his own goodness.

A Rat Tale

Unable to make you love me,
I chopped the tails off five live rats
and carried them with me everywhere I went
in a round snuff box.

I laid them on my polished oak table
in the shape of a star,
I slept with them under my duck-down pillow,
I floated them in my bath.

And in spite of my charms,
you didn't love me.

It was not until I cooked them
and took them into myself
like the holy body of Christ
that you looked on me more kindly.

Distance: Three Views

A short distance:
The opening between the front teeth
of a newborn pack rat
that fits exactly over the mother's nipple
and fills in when the baby is weaned.

A long distance:
The hundreds of light years between earth
and the North Star that, despite the staggering
number of miles, is measurable
by mathematicians or by an inch worm.

An incomprehensible distance:
The lonely stretch of heart,
the inconsolable ache,
the unspanable space
between lovers unwillingly apart.

Rite Of Purification

Your hands,
blue light,
they find small birds in my body
and illuminate them.

Your mouth,
sweet fastener,
relates to moss,
licorice fern roots,
sea creatures
that cling to wet rocks.

Joined
in earth, sea and air,
we laugh
to be so pure.

Jack Island, December

First snow across the bay,
and we two lean together
at the window

watching islands whiten,
lull. Our whispered words
are scraps that catch awhile

around the sill and then escape
through glass to blow away
in snow until, at last,

we speak no more
but enter touch entirely
and mingle

like the witching light
of islands blending,
into snow and sea.

The Rose

The morning Darrell went to the hospital,
Marc gave me a rose
from an abandoned garden.

There were five pink petals
of exquisite silk—
fragrant,
flawless,
wide-open—
the size of my palm.
And five perfect leaves—
carved by a Master's hand.

In the blossom's center,
delicate beige stamens
nodded and trembled.
My breath—I thought.
But no—
a fragile, half-transparent worm
traveled there—
searching,
tapping each anther
with his blind head,
threading oblivious
among the filaments.

It's All In Knowing
Where To Look Before Death

We sat together in the garden
watching with downcast eyes
the silent flow of tumbler pigeon shadows
glide and ghost across the grass.
And in that flat, dark dance
we found a certain two-dimensional delight.

But when we lifted up our eyes,
we were astonished at the sight
of sunlight through white wings
and fanned-out tails.
Stunned by seven angels doing air-ballet
above our garden.
They were tethered to our hearts,
and tugged us heavenward,
reminding us of other morning minions,
transporting us beyond mere shadows
to that sacred brilliance where there is no death.

Then Plato,
strolling somewhere on a marble stoa,
arched his eyebrows and adjusted his toga,
and Jesus,
that crusty old fisher,
chuckled like small thunder in the distance—
both too polite to say,
"I told you so."

Long Before Dawn

On this morning of your funeral,
I step into the dark garden
long before dawn
in search of comfort.

Anything,
wags and licks from the dogs,
but they are asleep
beside the door.

Perhaps, a rose
still blooming
on your favorite bush.
But, no,
and only half a moon
falling down the sky.

I startle at the black animal
creeping silently beside me.
My shadow
lonely
and singular.

HIGH WHITE MOON

Some Rites And A Sacrament For Darrell

The morning you died
to this dualistic world of suffering and joy,
everything was clear between us.
Clear as the air at dawn,
pure as water from the deepest spring.
And I lay down beside you,
and we fell into each other
understanding the truth of waves
rising out of the sea
and returning.

At last, we drew the Tibetan kahta
across your naked body, so you could slip away
under the peacefulness of silk.

Izumi* just missed your final breath
and, wailing, flung herself
across your body.
"But, Mother, Mother," she cried,
"Father's chest is still warm."
She insisted the mortician
take your best shoes.
"He has so many hills to climb.
And there's so much snow."

One son tucked a picture of himself
under your hand in that last boat,
another sent a fishing pole,
and your grandson, his best hand-tied fly.
I sent nothing but a bundle of memories:
moonlight across Samish Bay,

HIGH WHITE
MOON

the orchard in April,
walks in winter woods.

At the cemetery Izumi served hot saki
and poured some into the ground
where she thought your mouth would be.

That night I found
the last pomegranate you would ever bring
into this house
and held it in both my hands
like a leathery red heart.
I began kneading it with my thumbs,
popping the flesh around inner seeds.
One by one,
I felt the tenderness give way inside,
heard the sweetness tearing,
bursting into wine.
And when the fruit was juicy and full,
I opened the skin
and drank.

*Izumi, our adopted Japanese daughter, flew from Osaka.

Points Of View

The dove,
hawk-driven,
crashed into the north window
and fell to the walk below.
Neck bones severed on impact,
her head lolled like a rag doll,
and she lay useless in my hands.
Except to put her in the field
breast down, wings out
like a feathered cross.

That dove
has left her imprint on glass.
A fine white etching
of delicate feathers,
wings that reach upward
pointing out heaven.
Her eyes—my God—and bill,
even her feet are here on the pane.

"How can this be?" we ask.

"Imagine the speed."

"Perhaps she had just bathed in dust."

But the dove's death
is more than a simple happening
like food for a raptor,
or a dusty impression
of bird elegance.

It is a message from you
that imprints my heart.

Loneliness

Sick, all winter I am sick.
Spend my days lying in the window seat
watching birds.
No energy; flu that won't go;
I am waiting, suspended.

Reaching, I touch emptiness,
emptiness touches back.
My heart, a pomegranate
collapsed on itself.
My throat, choked by a chunk of apple.

An Arctic Express
blasts across the bay,
smashing ink-water to white
on island walls.

Sun,
a cold coin falling into its slot,
is low in ice-blue sky,
and pale moon,
slick as a surgeon's glove,
rises above stone.

It is a bitter wind that snarls
the long white hair of chimney smoke.

Kettle Burn

The steam scald was flagellation
not atonement.
No calvary but Van Gogh's ear.

Tender white of flesh beneath
the wrist was proffered to
the copper dragon spouting steam
the day you left.

Skin blushed and reddened,
raised a watery center
like a fluid daisy cushion
and petaled-out raw red.

After oil and pain
I wore the blossom quizzically
until it wrinkled, browned
and died.

Now, a shadow on my arm,
an outsized freckle,
reminds me what I did
and did not do.

Who Are You Tells Me This Dream

You rise up easily,
tenderly
and bend over me
to kiss.

Your lips
go to my throat,
to that shallow valley
where apple gets stuck,
where hurt can't be swallowed.

I think you will nuzzle
in that soft place,
but pinching my skin
between your teeth,
you bite.

You bite so hard
a flock of small silver birds
flies northward out of my mouth.

Glittering.

For The Sake Of Grace

Naked
silk tender
she walked among thorns.
Feet pierced
breasts bleeding.

People shouting
Get out
Get out
You'll be hurt.

Oh yes! she cried

and plunged deeper
into thicket.

Wounding

The soldier ran
his sword
into Christ's side.

And Christ,
knowing our need
for wounding,
sighed deeply
and blessed him.

Transformation

The poet heals herself:
sterilizes the gash over her heart
with strong spirits and salty tears.

Wipes deep into the cut
with Mother's bloody hankie
removing remnants
of broken promises
and other contaminants.

She sutures
with a darning needle
drawing ribbons
through tender flesh
and celebrates the closing.

Embellishes her wound
with shells and beads,
vermillion feathers,
a leper's bell sans clapper.

Letting Go

All day I practice letting go.
Pour milk slowly over oatmeal,
allow autumn wind to blow
one golden leaf from my hand,
refusing to hold on, though
part me me wants to crush it in my fist.
Neighbors come and go,
slip in and out as easily as silver air,
the phone,
raindrops, dolorous,
but freely weeping down the pane.
Deliberately, I drop my slippers
one by one beside the bed,
a grim relinquishing in cameo.

Then, doves pull out their feathers
in my dreams and drop them
down the night like snow,
and you gone, now, from my bed
reach out and touch my face
and say, "I know. I know."

Rose Metaphor

It is true that I had not been truly loved
until you loved me to a storm
that washed the raging sea around and through
and over me in whirling, pooled delight.

And when the fury of the winds that rocked us
wound their circles down,
we centered in the eye of our small hurricane.

And then it was, a rose
as round and pale as moon light,
bloomed my thighs.

And when I told you so,
it was as though you did not hear:
you did not speak or open your eyes.
You were embarrassed by my metaphor,
I thought,
and we lay quiet listening to the rain.

Next day, all out of context of the conversation,
astounding those around us—heaven knows—
you smiled-up suddenly, half-teasingly and asked,
"What color was that rose?"

HIGH WHITE MOON

FOR DARRELL
WHO TRAFFICKED WITH ANGELS

I drop my blue-eyed dream of you
into the eternal and infinite
ocean of shimmering possibilities
and you rise,
all golden and laughing,
to fold me in your wings.

SECTION IV

HONSHU ISLAND POEMS

Izumi Toda, a graduate of Kyoto University, came to stay with us for two weeks as she taught about Japanese culture at Anacortes High School. Through a comedy of cultural errors, she remained for four years. When she told us she did not want to marry the man her father had chosen for her in Japan, we suggested she write her father and tell him. Wrong thing to do. She was immediately disowned. A go-between called to tell her she had no family and no home.

Of course, we kept her here with us, and miracle of save-face miracles, after a couple of years her father's face began to mend. He was able to recover his dignity because our family had taken her in and cared for her. Otoasan (Father) was able to report this to his Japanese friends and they agreed he should welcome Izumi back to his family.

By then she was attending Skagit Valley College and we had become her American father and mother. Her family came here to visit. We went there to visit, and finally she returned to Japan to marry another man her father had chosen. This man was agreeable to her.

Darrell and I attended her wedding. After the Shinto ceremony she changed out of her traditional kimonos (there were four), and came into the reception wearing my wedding dress.

Trips to Japan have opened an oriental cultural delight and have been an inspiration for many poems.

HIGH WHITE MOON

The Rabbit In The Moon

In Japan grandmothers and grandfathers tell children about the rabbit who makes rice-cakes in the moon when families gather for moon-viewing in autumn.

Izumi goes on tiny running feet
that scuff-up whisper sounds within this house
and scatters laughter here the way that flower-girls
drop petals at a wedding, or cherry trees
in springtime float their blossoms on clear air.
Wearing jeans, she comforts men within these walls
just as her mother and her mother's mother
dressed in their kimonos gentled men
with merest bows and lovely little lies.

But she and I, we hold our hands upon our mouths
and giggle in the kitchen over jokes so subtle
they can only be translated through the heart
and eyes. And other times, when we don't know
the words to speak our feelings,
we fold them into paper cranes
and wear them around our necks.

Filled with amazement and delight
to find this Oriental spirit in my Northwest home
I ask, "Where do you come from, Izumi?"
"The Moon," she laughs.
"I make rice cakes in the Moon.
I am the Rabbit in the Moon."

Izumi

Izumi, love daughter,
small shining Buddha
come unbidden to our garden,
surprising as purple violets
beneath December snow.
"Izumi," in Japan and here
means "spring in winter,"
and "clear water fountaining
from deep below."

Izumi Tells Masaaki About American Parents Catching Guemes Ferry

Father does not like late.
He wants to go ferry dock one-half hour early.
Mother says,
"We can stop for coffee."

Father drives on.
Says, "No time."
Mother says,
"Izumi would like a strawberry cone."

"This is Friday,
there'll be too many cars."
Mother looks out window on her side.
Doesn't saying anything.

We are number two in line at dock
and Father says,
"It's a beautiful day."
Mother looks at her watch.
Says nothing.

Father says,
"Alan looks good.
His back must be better."
Mother looks up at seagulls.

Father says, "I have red bananas
in the trunk. Would you like one?"

After a long time Mother says,
"I might."

On Entering the Kingdom of Heaven

Peony Priest and I
sit lotused on tatami
in the Peony Temple.
Trying to say the unsayable,
I am caught, pinned
like a butterfly to the tiger screen.
"Stupid," I mumble,
I am stupid. Ignorant."
Peony Priest brightens,
bows almost imperceptibly,
"Yes, you are profoundly ignorant.
I am profoundly ignorant."

My eyes shut down,
my heart opens to the pale green of bamboo,
the wind-ruffled water of rice fields,
the fragrance of one thousand peonies.

But still I am troubled.
"I hate the word *ignorant* Flower Father."

"Children have another name for it," he smiles,
his eyes disappearing into golden flesh.
Half afraid to hear, I hesitate before I ask,
"What name?"

And then I become the bamboo,
the wind-ruffled water,
one thousand peonies
as he whispers,
"Innocent."

—For Daijyo Oota, Godo

ON BECOMING AN EMPRESS

The old car suspended
high under the temple rafters,
is not a Toyota or Honda.
It is a wooden car with no wheels.
Eight strong men were
the engine for this vehicle.

I crane upward,
astonished at black lacquer
covered with flowers, birds
and twining vines; it is a painted
garden hanging beneath the roof.

Peony Priest produces a ladder.
"Go up," he orders proud of himself
for having revealed such a treasure.

I "go up."
The ladder wobbles. It is high.

"Go in," he calls.
"The Emperor rode in it".

I squeeze in the small door
and barely fit. Suddenly,
I am an Empress in her private car;
a large doll with whitened face;
red circles on my cheeks.
My silk kimono blooms with peonies;
behind my back, a tiger springs.
My tiny painted lips are silent.
My downcast eyes assure subservience.

HIGH WHITE
MOON

Drawing back the curtain,
I flutter my small Empress fan,
and vow to ride demure and humble
all the way to Tokyo.
Far below,
Peony Priest, bobbing and bowing,
shouting, "Come down! Come down!"

On Visiting Peony Priest a Second Time

I have thought of the perfect present
for Peony Priest—an ostrich egg.
More perfect than any painting or poem;
the texture, the glaze, the color,
the oval shape, no beginning or ending.

And when I place it into his two hands,
I will say without speaking,
"Here is my poem, Peony Priest,
flawless and mute."

And he will know
and bow deeply
because of the purity.

HIGH WHITE MOON

Speaking Zen On Reflection

Peony Priest, kneeling by the pond,
watches night-stilled fish and reflected moon.
I kneel beside him, so close
the silk sleeves of our kimonos touch.
Now there are four in the dark mirror:
the Peony Priest, a silver-white koi,
the moon and I.

Everything is quiet in the temple garden
except crickets scraping small violins,
and fireflies flickering among the leaves.

He sees me reflected in the water,
but does he know
I am at his side as well?

At last, I say, "Daijyo-san, it is so beautiful."

He does not answer.

Only the pond.

The next morning, a white peony arrives.

"From Peony Priest," the small boy chirps.

I send him running back through rice fields
with my best breakfast egg.

Watching Otoasan Tend Bonsai

I could never grow bonsai
exquisite as they are:
could not snip and prune a pine,
always watching for new growth
to be nipped
in the nick of time;
could not count the drops of water
so there would be
just enough to sustain life;
could not keep a tree
tiny and perfect on a low table
for a hundred years.

My houseplants grow
wild and lush
in rich and damp manures,
spilling from pots,
climbing walls,
reaching all day and night.
They do not live as long as bonsai
but—oh the glory of green leaves
bursting through the house
leaning into light.

Japanese Women And Their Sons

Sitting on tatami with three attendants
Baby Junichi sucks
one fat noodle at a time
into his tiny mouth that is pursed
as for a whistle.
Eight to ten inches long,
the noodles disappear noiselessly,
slip into him without interruption
until the bowl is empty.
When Auntie hands him to his mother,
 he lifts her shirt and nurses
until the milk puddles in the corner
of his mouth.
Then, "Pah Pah!" he cries—
his name for the blanket sling
that Auntie and Mother use
to secure him
to Grandmother's back.

As Grandmother works
bending, rocking, swaying—
Junichi becomes a part of her body—
a fat sleeping baby
not yet delivered from his ancestors.

Woman As Hare*

American women
who grew up asleep in the arms
of the *Ladies Home Journal,*
who have played second fiddle
all their lives
deferring to husbands and sons,
these women dream hares.

Smoke-gray animals
motionless and wide-eyed
in the middle of a burning field
patiently awaiting flames,
the smell of burned fur and flesh.
Resigned.

Japanese women
who grew up asleep on the backs
of their mothers,
who have dropped to their knees,
bowed so low to husbands and sons
that their foreheads touched tatami,
these women also dream hares.

They lift the sacrificial animal
by its ears and slit its throat.
Red-black blood gushes
like a small river,
and the hare does not mind.

*Hares are known to freeze and wait motionless for death in a burning field and often appear in dreams as the archetype of self-sacrifice.

Learning About Heaven

In Japan old women
bend forward at the waist,
point their sun bonnets
toward the cabbages and rice
just after dawn.
Half a day later,
they leave to make dinner,
and cannot straighten all the way
but lean toward home
like small trees
misshapen by persistent winds.
Clasping their hands
behind their backs for balance,
their eyes ever earthward,
they see the shadows
of high birds beneath them on the path,
the reflection of sun and cloud
fallen into rice-field waters.

In Japan, old women learn of heaven
through bowing to the earth.

Two Women Under Cherry Blossoms

Hatsuie and I speak and bow,
bob three times like two large birds
greeting each other after a long separation.

She, bent forward at the waist
from years in the rice field;
I, a little wobbly yet
from jet lag.

How glad we are to see each other
here under cherry blossoms
in a light rain.
We speak, in turn, of weather
and grandchildren:
she in Japanese,
I in English,
neither understanding a word
the other says,
yet understanding each other perfectly.

When a breeze stirs blossoms,
pink petals fall onto our hair,
bless us as we talk,
as we caress each other with our sounds.

And when we part,
we bow so deeply
that our heads touch at the crown.

HIGH WHITE
MOON

Photo by Dixon Elder

Thelma J. Palmer has always lived on islands which she thinks of as "eye-lands," places where there is much to be seen and learned. Although she travels widely, she has never resided more than twenty miles from the house where she was born on Fidalgo Island in the San Juan Archipelago. For the past twenty years she has made her home on the small adjacent island of Guemes. Each year she visits Honshu Island in Japan.

Her first book of poetry is *The Sacred Round: Poems from an Island garden*. Her poems, articles and short stories have appeared in The English Journal, In Context, Organic Gardening, Family Circle, Fine Gardening, Wholistic Living News, Jeopardy, Bellingham Review and Reader's Digest. Her other books are *Enchantment of the World: France* coauthored with British historian Peter Moss and *Long Journey to the Rose Garden*.